The genuine article

*A*fter the exhilarating first flush of freedom and frolic that lightens a fresher's heart, head and bank balance, two depressing realities swiftly threaten to spoil the party. One is the shocking discovery that there really *is* nobody else to cook your meals/scrub your smalls/get you out of bed before midday. The other is that you have to research and write lengthy essays for a bunch of wretched academics who hold your future in their scrawny hands.

The good news is that time or revolted room-mates will soon solve the reheated porridge/sweaty sock problem. The bad news is that writer's block, however commonly experienced, is not a recognised campus disease. Unlike the soiled undies, folks, it just won't wash.

Generations of students have spent futile weeks attempting to avoid this grim reality, by which time most of a term has elapsed amid a rash of poor marks and snide marginal scrawlings by weary tutors who have witnessed the tragi-comedy year after year.

Enter GOOD ESSAYS, which assumes that you've never done any serious writing before, and which takes you through the essential stages of reading, planning and composition so that you hit the ground running.

We're not going to insult your intelligence by preaching the obvious. Essay guides are prone to suggesting that you get plenty of sleep (did these guys never room next to the mad saxophonist or the ever-flushing lavatory?); that you fix yourself a sensible diet (did *they* feel like eating after ten pints of cider and blackcurrant the night before?); and that you sit down to work in a comfortable, well-lit room (did they ever live on campus, for Provost's sake?).

What GOOD ESSAYS attempts to do, on the other hand, is to tackle the genuine difficulties - of which thinking clearly is perhaps the greatest. We'll help you to use your reading and marshal your thoughts in well-structured essays that know where they're going.

Go on: make the grade!

Read! read! read!

A Fact Of University Life (FOUL) vital to take on board at the outset is that academics in the social sciences and humanities approach everything through books.

What this means is that, however brilliant your mind may be, you're bound to fail if you don't show evidence of reading.

But what, you cry, if I happen to have the insights of a Foucault, the transformative genius of a Derrida, the all-encompassing grasp of a Hawking?

Sorry, but that's not quite enough!

A subsidiary FOUL is that your tutors will themselves have read a vast amount.

This means that they'll recognise the bits you quote; that they'll have a shrewd idea where you picked them up if it's not from the original work; and that they'll know when you're faking.

There is, unfortunately, no substitute for the grind (which may sometimes surprise you as a pleasure) of reading as much as you can lay your hands on.

WITHDRAWN
GOOD
ESSAYS

*how to plan them
and to write them*

Ann Varley

Pomegranate
Practicals

"Tell you everything you need to know
- and leave out everything you don't'

Dr Ann Varley is a lecturer in geography at University College
London. David Arscott is a writer and broadcaster, and author of
the Pomegranate *Good English* guide.

British Library Cataloguing-in-Publication Data.
A catalogue record for this book is available from the British Library.

ISBN 0 9533493-1-4

Published by Pomegranate Press,
Church Cottage, Westmeston, Hassocks, Sussex BN6 8RH
Telephone/fax: 01273 846743
E-mail: 106461.1316@compuserve.com

Printed in England by M.D. Morgan, Red Lake Terrace, Ore,
Hastings, Sussex TN35 4JR (01424) 437741

You really want to know what *I* think?

The word 'originality' is liable to scare the mortar boards off students who regard themselves as conscientious enough (when the mood takes them) but uninspired - in other words all but the most arrogant of us when we begin our little adventure in academia.

You'll quickly learn that tutors give good marks to those who display this magical quality, and poor marks to those who don't, but you're likely to ask yourself how you can possibly be original when you only began to study the damned subject in earnest a couple of weeks ago.

Is there a catch?

The short answer is No, while the longer (and ridiculously-far-fetched-but-do-try-to-bear-with-us) answer is Remember Shakespeare.

The Bard, you may recall, unashamedly borrowed the plots of his plays, his outlandish originality lying elsewhere.

You won't, mercifully, be required to knock up a few sonnets or a tragedy, but you *will* find plenty of 'plots' to work on in the books you read. Without turning your hand to literary flourish you'll be expected

Don't be sheepish - originality isn't another word for glittering genius

to take the substance of what you find in all those books on your reading list - plus a few more if you really want to earn some brownie points - and remould it into something new.

All right: *sort of* new. You can happily assume that you will discover nothing in these first few anguished weeks which has remained hidden from great minds over years and perhaps centuries. What your tutor is looking for is evidence that you have not only raided the library for the texts but have thought about them, too.

Shaping and reorganising things your way constitutes originality.

Originality

The importance of reading a good deal will rapidly become apparent to you. If you've consulted only one authority you'll find it nigh on impossible to do anything but parrot it - with a high risk of plagiarism (*see p 27*).

A Funny Thing Happened on My Way to the Lecture Theatre . . .

But, unfortunately, your tutor won't wish to hear about it in the pages of your essay.

Does that mean that personal comment is banished?

No! This is your original piece of work. Your views (and more rarely your experiences) may therefore legitimately find a place within it PROVIDED THAT THEY ARE 100% RELEVANT.

The word 'I' won't be frowned upon as long as you demonstrate that you are thoroughly immersed in your material and are making a carefully considered judgement based on a wide range of evidence.

What you should be careful NOT *to do is to end a well argued essay with an airy personal comment which over-simplifies or trivialises a complex problem: 'In my opinion, the way to stop global warming is to ban motor vehicles' or 'the solution to global poverty is to cancel third world debt'.*

Once you have a few texts under your belt you'll begin to discover how broad and deep your subject can be. (You'll also, no doubt, despair of its complexity, but that's something we'll deal with later.)

This, of course, is where you start to worry all over again. How can little old you possibly adjudicate between the brilliantly argued, but diametrically opposed, views of Professors X and Y over sexual initiation practices in Milton Keynes/the punctuation of Jack Kerouac/the rôle of the bed bug in western civilisation.

You can't, just yet. And if you *were* to dismiss one argument as absurd the chances are that your reasoning would seem pretty trite. These poor people, after all, have spent a long time in dark and dusty rooms with only a guttering candle for company.

What you *should* do is explore the evidence each brings to the debate. If one argument seems more persuasive than the other you should certainly say so - as long as you're moved by serious scholarship rather than blind prejudice.

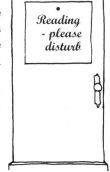

Reading - please disturb

So you've read all round the subject, and the ideas are careering around your brain like crazy. Now's the time to start . . .

Getting into a bit of an argument

The most common criticism of student essays (apart, that is, from their being late, illegible and unintelligible) is that they lack 'structure'.

Getting the structure right is so important that we shall be devoting several pages to it, but we'll first isolate the root cause of this sorry lack of organisation: the want of an 'argument' or sense of direction.

If you're averagely diligent you'll eventually reach the tremulous stage of planning your essay with a few reference books and a sheaf of useful notes *(see page 9)* at your elbow. You'll have decided what the main points are, and you'll have the evidence to illustrate them.

Then what?

Think, for a moment, of the essay as a journey. It's a Saturday, and you're about to set off on one of those interminably boring family occasions. You have to visit Aunty Gladys fifty miles up the road and

Uncle Luke, who lives just round the corner from her but has refused to speak to her ever since her cat ate his canary.

On the way you have to stop off at your local newsagents for a box of Aunty's favourite peppermint creams and at the antiquarian bookseller ten miles up the road who's managed to find Uncle a rare edition of Welding for Beginners.

On a good day you manage to call in everywhere in the right order. *(A well-structured journey.)* On a bad day you remember the book only as you're leaving Aunty, so that you have an extra round trip of 80 miles unless you want to be written out of Uncle's will. *(A badly-constructed journey.)*

On a really lousy day you go for a spin just to keep everyone happy, but neither they nor you know where you might end up. Aunty or Uncle may get a visit, but it's pot luck. *(No sense of direction.)*

5

Q: "Popeye became the archetypal urban hero because he ate lots of spinach." Discuss.

A Introduction: concept of the urban hero
- notion of urban hero overused (cf super-model): now means little more than the latest comic book figure to appear
- originally urban hero was a working class streetwise survivor

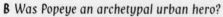

B Was Popeye an archetypal urban hero?
- described as such in contemporary sources: opinion polls, women's magazines etc
- possible rivals (Superman, Batman) - but none has achieved the same lasting fame

C Did Popeye become an urban hero because he ate spinach?

C1) Do we know that he ate a lot of spinach?
- direct evidence surprisingly thin - limited to famous scene in 1954 film 'Popeye Goes to Town'
- new archival research shows tins of spinach figured high on his shopping lists

C2) Does eating spinach make you an urban hero?
Reasons 'for':
a) it helps build the necessary muscle (see G. Grimshaw's article in The Nutritionist, Volume 6 No. 4 - 'Spinach and the macho male')
b) it tastes awful so you have to be a hero to stomach it
Reasons 'against':
a) Grimshaw's thesis contested by Nogreens in The nutritionist, Vol 7 No 2 - 'Spurious spinach: a reply to Grimshaw'
b) the spinach diet has connotations of quiche-eating vegetarianism

D If eating spinach was NOT the cause of Popeye's heroic status, to what other characteristics might we attribute this?
- in an era when masculinity was defined as the ability to beat up a rival, Popeye transcended the stereotype by showing that he had emotions. It is Olive Oil who makes him an urban hero, by making him the New Man before his time

Argument

We've already taken the analogy far enough, but we trust that you get our drift. The argument is a thread of reasoning that runs through your essay, giving it coherence and direction.

Without this discipline you're very likely to find yourself giving a couple of examples in favour of a particular theory followed by a couple against and then a couple more in favour. The bewildered reader is lost.

You'll understand from our essay plan on the opposite page (Popeye enthusiasts must forgive us for knowing little of his true life and times) why it is that your reading needs to be as deep and varied as time and sanity will allow.

There is, we emphasise, no one correct answer to an essay question or one single correct thread of argument. Indeed *(see p. 19)*, the straightforward narrative approach we've used here won't always be either possible or appropriate. What's important is that you can pick your way among a variety of texts and commentaries, coming up with a cogent and well-supported thesis.

To achieve this, you'll need to stand back from your material for a while. Dive in, and you're likely to produce what amounts to little more than a list of undigested thoughts and quotations: the dire shopping list approach.

Write down what you think are the three or four *major* themes and, as in our Popeye example, consider how they relate to one another: devise a logical pattern of argument to hold them together.

Now make a list of a few *minor* themes, and fit them into the overall pattern. If the various parts of the jigsaw just won't fit together you'll have to reshape your argument. No sweat: this is a relatively painless part of the exercise.

Finally, select from your notes the specific information and quotations you wish to use and decide where they will best fit into your narrative.

> *"Sir, I have found you an argument, but I am not obliged to find you an understanding"*
>
> **Dr Johnson**
> **Boswell's 'Life'**

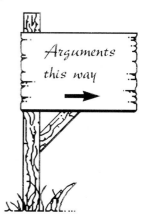

7

Beware the Internet, my son!
The megabite, the trawls that catch!
Beware the World Wide Web,
              and shun
The frumious Infosnatch!

*I*t's a fascinating world out there in cyberspace, but you shouldn't need us to tell you that some of its inhabitants would give Lewis Carroll's Jaberwock a close fight in a weirdo contest.

If you're cynical by nature you'll perhaps suspect that your tutors' doubts about the material you download from the Net may have something to do with the fact that they have no control over it. How can they judge whether the author of the report you cite is a fully-fledged academic (like respectable them) or a nutcase with a mission?

A moment's reflection should tell you that these timorous doubts are reasonable. Sources other than academic journals and books *may*, of course, be properly used in your essays, but you need to remember that there's precious little quality control on the Net.

Ask yourself who's publishing this material. The URL (address to you and me) is a pretty good guide to the sort of institution which owns the web pages you're reading. Academic institutions in the UK will have *ac.uk* as part of their URL, while those in the US will end *.edu*.

Most well-known organisations will give their name prominence in their address: the World Bank, to take one example, is at *http://www.worldbank.org/*. You may happen to loathe the World Bank and all it stands for, but it is at least staffed by intelligent people who are answerable for what they do.

Our tip, in short, is to be extremely wary of citing an individual or an organisation if you've never heard of them before.

Marshalling arts

Condensing what you read into note form is an invaluable exercise in selecting what's important

A **major difference between pre-university essays and those which are about to plague you is that your sweet old school teachers probably spoonfed you, handing you snippets of text on convenient photocopied sheets.**

Luxury! Now you must seek out a large building on the campus which, although it has the word LIBRARY emblazoned upon its austere front, is rarely discovered by new students for several weeks.

In it you will find large quantities of books and journals, but always just one too few of the title that you and your fellow inmates are all looking for. Camping outside overnight as for the January sales is regarded as nerdish, so the best bet is simply to be as prompt as possible this side of eagerness.

And then hunt the shelves for an additional volume or two. You won't wish to read everything from cover to cover, but you're looking for a range of books to give your research breadth and variety.

Which brings us to the subject of reliability. The texts to which you're directed by your tutors can be assumed to be worthy of serious consideration, but those you find for yourself - and hats off to you for initiative - need to be approached with care. *(See facing page.)*

We can't over-emphasise the need to Read Read Read, but that doesn't mean that you have to do nothing but Write Write Write. Taking notes is a skilled business, and learning the techniques will save you headaches later on.

The first tip is to avoid getting too much down at the outset. You can't be sure just yet how much of what you're reading will be invaluable, how much of it will appear in different guises in every book and how much is going to be plain useless to you. Copying out large, undigested chunks of material won't help you sort the wheat from the chaff.

If in doubt, leave it out!

Understanding what an argument is all about should help your winnowing. What you're looking for in your reading, remember, are major ideas and the quotations to illustrate them.

The spider plan

*(but if you're arachnaphobic,
feel free to look the other way)*

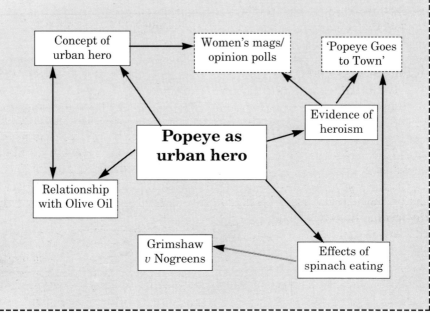

Using your reading

These notes are going to be the basic source for your essays.

Allow for the fact that you may not come back to your crude scribblings for several days, or even weeks. Make sure not only that your writing is legible to your slightly older self, but that you'll have no trouble finding the references again among all your source material: note the book title, author and page number.

Although your initial notes will inevitably be somewhat disordered, the time will come (and much too soon) when you need to marshal your research in order to write that wretched essay.

One ploy is to create charts and diagrams, though it has to be admitted that these suit some subjects, assignments and temperaments better than others.

Fatter text books than ours are often a geometrician's delight, but we shall limit ourselves to the spider chart on the opposite page, which has the benefit of pointing up in diagrammatic form the relationship of one idea to another. It's particularly useful for those projects which feature results and implications.

A simpler system is the linear list, which has the advantage of differentiating between your major and minor themes very clearly..

For example:

URBAN HERO
- what it means
- concept overused
  (comic books, ref.
Smith *et al*, 'Supermen'
p.4)

WAS POPEYE A HERO?
- Women's mags
  ("How P. changed my life": 'Woman's Realm', Jones p. 48)
- Rivals (*i.e.* Batman)

DID HE EAT SPINACH?
'Popeye Goes to Town'

'HEROIC SPINACH'
For:
- muscle building
(Grimshaw v. Nogreens)
Against:
- wimpy vegetarianism

OTHER REASONS FOR POPEYE'S STATUS
- Olive Oil
  ('Modern Trends', p 13)

Choose a method that you're comfortable with. Diagrams aren't essential, but clear thinking is.

Lecture notes

Whether that moist-eyed gaze you fix upon your lecturers is provoked by stifling boredom or shameless animal lust, do stir yourself into jotting down the gist of what they have to say. The most inspirational of performances is otherwise likely to remain in the memory as an accomplished vaudeville act with not a word to show for it.

Thrilled to be writing your own essay question? Don't be too easy on yourself . . .

You can hardly believe it when your tutor suggests that you come up with your own title for the essay you're preparing to write. What a splendid chance to concentrate on the things you know and to ignore those you don't!

WARNING!

Beware. We've already explored the need for an argument. What you have to avoid is a question which really isn't a question at all.

If, for example, you've immersed yourself in the novels of Charles Dickens and been fascinated by the various roles that money plays - to empower, persuade, corrupt and so on - you should NOT call your essay: Dickens and Money.

A title like that will encourage you merely to list all the references to money you can find, with no structure to your essay at all. Find one that puts you on your argumentative mettle: "Dickens is disgusted by the power of money" *or* "Money and vice are always linked in Dickens" *or* "Dickens shares the Victorian fascination with inherited wealth" - Discuss.

Decoding those ? cryptic clues

NOT highly recommended

A renowned (if, one reluctantly suspects, apocryphal) question in a Philosophy Finals exam at Oxford ran to a single word: WHY?

One particularly confident student is supposed to have answered this with the return question WHY NOT? - and to have been awarded a First.

While this is (just) credible, you should rest assured that our Smart Alec undergraduate must otherwise have answered the full quota of questions to a high standard.

Examiners may have a sense of humour, but they usually have the last laugh.

If the question looks simple, it could be that you haven't read it properly

No, they're not really intended to catch you out, but essay questions demand a great deal more attention than many students are inclined to grant them.

Casually run your eye over them, and it may seem obvious what's required of you. Read them again, with close attention, and you'll see that you've been given a set of clues to decipher.

The wording of the question should suggest both the structure of your essay and the weight you attach to the various elements within it.

As with crossword puzzles - but they're not quite *that* mind-bendingly devious - you need to understand their special language if you're to do yourself justice.

Unlike crossword puzzles, unfortunately, there are no handy little squares to fill in. Why? *a.* because your tutors enjoy the thought of you labouring through the long and tearful night (why should they be the only ones with guttering candles?), and *b.* there is (again) no right/wrong answer.

Think of a question as a way of stopping you from writing down everything you know. *(See our warning on the facing page.)* Instead, you must SELECT.

Understanding the question

These are some of the common codewords in essay questions:

Discuss.

The most basic of them all. It requires you to look at two sides of a question and to come to a conclusion - which is what a tutor in the social sciences or the humanities will virtually always want you to do. The two sides may not always be straightforward, but beware a simplistic approach.

"The chief cause of English working class solidarity was the influence of the mother" - Discuss may appear straightforward, but, should you disagree with the statement, you could easily find yourself led into a discussion of the other contributory factors, excluding the mothers altogether. Not, surely, what was intended.

Compare & contrast

Emphasises that there are likely to be different elements in the two sides of the question. *(See page 19)*

Assess the evidence for/
Evaluate the argument that

Beware giving strings of evidence without any value judgement.

Illustrate

Dangerous, because it doesn't lend itself to an obvious structure. Don't produce a shopping list.

A few tips:

• Use a dictionary.

Look up the meaning of any words which you don't know - or only 'sort of' know. It's surprising (well, it *used* to be) just how many students end up writing about the wrong thing entirely. Make it a *large* dictionary.

> "Them that asks no questions isn't told a lie"
>
> **Rudyard Kipling**
> *'A Smuggler's Song'*

• Brainstorm.

Open your mind to any crazy half-relevant idea that flits across your brain and jot it down. Then hack out the rubbish when you're feeling sober and efficient.

• Stand the question on its head.

Popeye was the last person you could call an urban hero. Odd, maybe, but seeing things the other way about can prove illuminating.

• Ask your tutor.

An outlandish idea, we agree, but it does sometimes work.

Tutors are always complaining about getting lost in student essays. Give your writing a logical structure and they'll have to think up some other reason for failing you

A route through the mental maze

We're not taught Logic at school, so it's hardly surprising that it takes some of us a little time to get into the academic frame of mind.

The lesson may be especially hard to learn in the Arts field, where it's tempting to kid yourself that, since you're not one of those hard-nosed Maths & Science types, you can safely allow 'ideas' and feelings to stand in for rigorous consequential thinking.

Not true!

To write a first-class essay which has your tutor purring takes skill as well as effort, and the building of a logical framework is a vital part of the job.

By the time you've finished, after all, you'll have covered a variety of related topics, throwing out thoughts and bringing in references from numerous different sources.

Even if you've expressed yourself in language of the greatest clarity, it will be unusual if your absent-minded reader doesn't occasionally have to check how you managed to get from point A to point B. If the leap was a false one, your tutor will begin scribbling in the margin.

You've already taken

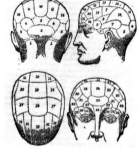

the first steps towards organising your essay material: you've read your books, taken your notes and sorted out your major and minor themes.

Now an awful truth will dawn upon you. However satisfyingly elaborate your charts and diagrams may be, however efficient the way in which you've cross-referenced this idea to that, the actual writing of the essay involves ordering your thoughts sequentially, one sentence after another. And another.

You can't, as you may have done in your notes, use capital letters here, and circles there and arrows all over the place. All those complex relationships between themes and ideas have to be built up step by step - and

yet still, somehow, form themselves into patterns which separate major from minor, broad sweep from tiny detail.

Yes, folks, you've remembered what we're after: a good old ARGUMENT!

Argument may, if you're lucky, itself suggest the structure

of your essay. Our Popeye essay outline on page 6 assumes that you have an impressively wide range of references at your disposal (you've read a lot) and that the nature of the question enables you to examine the various themes in a straight-forward order before

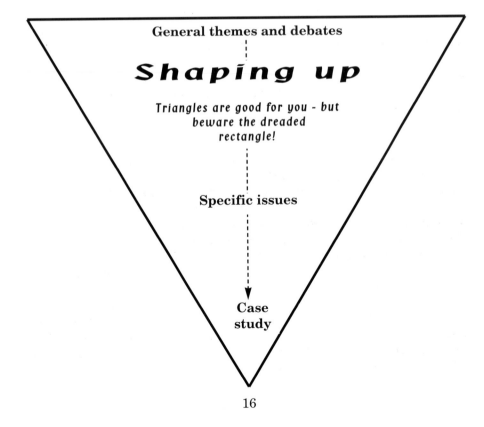

General themes and debates

Shaping up

Triangles are good for you - but beware the dreaded rectangle!

Specific issues

Case study

reaching an amply justified conclusion. You've moved confidently from A to E, citing sound evidence at every stage.

Unfortunately, this simple structure isn't always possible, either because of what the question asks or because the material you bring to the essay doesn't allow it.

If this is the case you'll have to think of some other way of ordering your material so that it nevertheless still manages to develop your argument in a logical, comprehensible fashion. You need a shape!

Triangles

The diagram on the facing page depicts a structure which may suit your purposes: the triangle.

The wider part of the triangle represents broad, general themes, while the narrower part is concerned with specifics.

An essay which dealt with nothing but the broad themes would lose heavily for showing no evidence of detailed reading. An essay made up of fine detail would lose marks for having no intellectual grasp.

> "Contrariwise," continued Tweedledee, "it if was so, it might be: and if it were so, it would be: but as it isn't, it ain't. That's logic."
> Lewis Carroll
> 'Through the Looking Glass'

These, dear reader, are *rectangles* and are to be despised.

You shouldn't, on the other hand, career madly from broad stroke to pointillist detail and back again - which is why that triangle is so useful.

Broad to narrow

Let's imagine that you're totally immersed in that 1954 Popeye film, but aren't so hot on the general theory: all you have are your lecture notes.

You could use those notes to provide the broad part of the triangle, but could then legitimately say (perhaps a third of the way into the essay) something like this: 'In the following pages I provide a detailed analysis of one specific example, the 1954 film Popeye Goes to Town.

'This case study is especially relevant because it has been called the classic Popeye film. We shall see the themes I have already mentioned emerging in my discussion of it.'

Narrow to broad

Here you might start with a discussion of the film, or even of a particular scene within it, broadening out to show how it is relevant to the essay question.

Structure

SIGNPOSTS

However logical the structure of your essay may be, it's important to emphasise the flow of your argument by erecting 'signposts' along the way.

These are the simple words that give the reader a nudge about what you're up to.

If you've a number of lengthy points to make on a single theme, you might preface each of them with 'first', 'secondly', and 'thirdly' to make it clear when you're moving on.

'Thus', 'therefore' and 'consequently' stress logical progression (but do make sure that the logic is genuine); while 'however', 'despite' and 'nonetheless' mark a contrast.

Phrases such as 'having dealt with' and 'before considering' are useful for separating one set of ideas from another.

Don't overdo it, but think of your reader as a weary hiker without a map, a good sense of direction or a great deal of patience.

Now you might say: 'I shall demonstrate in the rest of my essay that by analysing a single scene in this film we can see 1. that Popeye is shown as an urban hero [in the following ways]; 2 that he is shown eating bowl after bowl of spinach after which his muscles bulge; 3. that the role of Olive Oil is clearly important, therefore etc etc.'

Hourglasses

As we've said, you shouldn't lurch from the broad to the narrow with giddy insouciance (actually we didn't put it quite as well last time), but another favoured shape is the hourglass. It is, when you think about it, just one of our illustrated triangles with an inverted one below it.

You might like first to consider the general themes; then to focus on the film scene for specific examples; and finally to move out again to draw wider conclusions from what you have seen in the film.

There isn't, as ever, a single correct answer to the structure problem, but you do need to give it serious thought before you start.

Keep asking yourself if this is the logical way of presenting your argument. Would anyone ignorant of the subject readily make sense of it? (This takes some honesty, because at two o'clock in the morning it's tempting to ignore that little inner voice which pipes up with uncomfortable questions.)

If you discover that there's a flaw in your logic, keep p l a y i n g around with the structure until the ideas flow with a quite irresistible momentum.

18

Structure

It may be, of course, that arrows, triangles and hourglasses all fail to meet the demands of your particular essay, and this is likely to be the case with one of the COMPARE & CONTRAST type questions.

These are often hideously complex at first glance, and *(see above right)* don't necessarily have the words 'compare' or 'contrast' in them at all. What they demand is some deft juggling of diverse material: a clear line of argument is rarely apparent at first sight.

We've chosen Richmond Park and Hampstead Heath as the open spaces - two are the least you can get away with.

First, of course, do your research and note-taking. We suggest *(right)* a useful way of keeping tabs on the dizzying range of material you're busily amassing.

SAMPLE 'COMPARE & CONTRAST' TYPE QUESTION:

"With reference to places you have visited, consider the relationship between past and present in the conservation of open spaces in London."

Decide, as you're reading, on your main themes or concepts, and then tick off the work you've done on each case in the past and the present. The workplan alerts you to gaps in your reading.

These themes - which mark your originality, don't forget - should:

• Emerge from your reading and your observations.
• Relate to both of your examples.
• Relate to both past and present.
• Be relevant to conservation.

Eventually, of course, you'll have to decide how to turn a detailed

Workplan	Case 1 RICHMOND PARK		Case 2 HAMPSTEAD HEATH	
Themes	past	present	past	present
OWNERSHIP		✓	✓	
LEGAL REGULATIONS	✓	✓		
MANAGEMENT TECHNIQUES				✓
etc				

19

chart into a logical, consecutive account. Which comes first: the themes, the cases or past *versus* present?

Two sound solutions:

Version A

THEME 1 (Ownership)
  (i) past of case 1
  (ii) past of case 2
  (iii) present of case 1
  (iv) present of case 2
THEME 2 (Regulations)
  (i) (ii) (iii) (iv) as
before.
THEME 3 (Management)
  (i) (ii) (iii) (iv)
Do keep the order of the sites the same!

Predictable, you may think, but an intuitive approach would get you into all sorts of trouble. Even if *you* know where you're going, your hapless tutor won't.

Version B

THEME 1
  (i) past of case 1
  (ii) present of case 1
  (iii) past of case 2
  (iv) present of case 2
(Then THEMES 2, 3 etc)

In both **A** and **B** the argument is well structured. A good mark will depend upon the quality of your argument, but at least you'll carry your reader with you.

And what NOT to do:

Version C

CASE 1 - all you know *(even if arranged by themes, with a consistent arrangement of past and present etc)*
CASE 2 - ditto.

Version D

CASE 1 - chronological account of all you know, with no regard for question, themes, past/present contrast
CASE 2 - ditto

✳ **Chronologies are OUT. It's not a story they want, but analysis, analysis, analysis.**

Sending in the Paras

If you're not used to report or essay writing you'll very soon discover that all those exciting ideas you're weaving in tendril-like sentences across the page will rapidly spread into an impenetrable jungle where no birds sing.

The answer is to break your writing up into PARAGRAPHS - although *not* wherever the fancy takes you.

Paragraphs are another (and a major) form of logical signposting, indicating a development of the argument or a change of direction. They can be as short as a single sentence or as long as a page, but they generally fall somewhere between these extremes.

The best bet for a beginner is to see how the professionals do it. Take up those texts you've been consulting and single-mindedly scan them for their paragraph-making.

Some tutors in some subjects will encourage you to use SUB-HEADS as directional signs, highlighting the main themes.

Fine - but do get the paragraph structure right first.

Larkin may have been right about the modern novel, but with essays it's sometimes the other way about - a sound argument is let down by feeble . . .

Beginnings & endings

If it's agony getting those first words down on the page, it can seem blissfully simple to round the whole thing off with a rhetorical flourish.

Both ends of your essay, however, require careful thought - the opening because it sets the tone and direction of your writing; the closing because it makes an impression out of all proportion to the number of words involved.

A straightforward way of starting is to make a general summary of the argument you're about to pursue: *Popeye is known for his strength and guile, but his success as an urban hero depends less on the muscle-building effects* of spinach than on his unexpected ability to challenge male stereotypes of the time.

Having made this 'statement of intent', you can follow your essay plan from the beginning, as your reader has now got the drift of what you're going to say.

The alternative is to begin with a specific fact on which you then build: *In the film Popeye Goes to Town our 'archetypal urban hero' acts aggressively whenever he eats spinach.*

Your reader won't immediately know the route ahead, but that won't matter as long as your essay is logical and well-signposted throughout.

> "Far too many relied on the classic formula of a beginning, a muddle, and an end"
>
> **Philip Larkin, 'New Fiction'**

Not the dratted dictionary again!
Resist the temptation to begin your essay with a dictionary definition: *'According to the OED, an urban hero is . . .'* This is old hat, very boring - and doesn't get you very far at all.

Endings

Endings may appear to write themselves, but they don't. Sure, if you've conducted a good argument your reader will know pretty well where you stand, but that's no excuse for a weak throw-away line.

If you've begun with that general summary, you can't repeat it, but you might nevertheless draw things together in a slightly different way: *Popeye himself might not have recognised his indebtedness to Olive Oil rather than the iron-rich vegetable, but the weight of evidence makes her influence indisputable.*

The important thing is to create a genuine conclusion, rather than simply to sink into exhaustion, the pen (or mouse) falling from your limp, enervated grasp.

And some don'ts:

● Don't simply repeat the question in the answer: *Therefore we see that Popeye became/did not become the archetypal urban hero because he ate spinach.* This is trite - and won't earn extra marks from teacher.

● Don't introduce new points. *In a recent survey, incidentally, Popeye was found to be the best-known sailor, real or fictional, in America.* Ah, you've just discovered that note and think it's too good a point to leave out. Perhaps, but the conclusion certainly isn't the place for it.

BUT a brief comment which changes the perspective is welcome: *The much-vaunted effects of spinach-eating are therefore seen to be peripheral, whereas the well-documented influence of Olive Oil is generally unsung - a reflection, perhaps, of the kind of society which feels the need for urban heroes in the first place.* This doesn't run counter to what you have already written, but leaves a tantalising but relevant (you hope) thought in the reader's mind.

● Don't suddenly lurch into the personal: *I loathe the masculine stupidity of the Popeye stereotype.* Your originality, remember, lies in your argument - which, in turn, relies upon sound evidence. What you feel is otherwise of interest only to your loved ones, your shrink and the (eventual) readers of your best-selling memoirs.

● Don't try to prove something that you haven't: *Popeye can therefore be seen as a genuine fore-runner of Nineties New Man.* Is that really what you were arguing? And have you provided the evidence to support the conclusion?

Mind your language!

You may not be too bothered about it, but slipshod English drives those tutors mad

You may be tempted to guffaw when the old fogies get sniffy about the way you handle (or mishandle, or manhandle) the English language.

For some strange reason they tend to come down hard on essayists who demonstrate incompetence in using their own mother tongue.

The reason for their harshness isn't, of course, hard to determine. Clear thinking is the essence of academic excellence, and if you can't put your thoughts into decent shape, you haven't a chance.

This isn't the place for a grammar lesson - we have *(see page 30)* a separate pocket guide for that - but here are a few of the things that tend to get up donnish noses.

• Waffle

Nothing is more obvious to the tutor than playing-for-time, round-the-houses language which is pure padding, with no real information but yards of pseudo opinions which suggest an insight the writer doesn't possess. It is, indeed, possible to write several dozen lines at a time without really saying anything, but they'll know.

• Pomposity

An allied vice. Use the simplest words that do the job - you won't be teaching your tutor any new words. (That's for the bar afterwards.) Cut out superfluous phrases such as 'It may be considered that' which have been stuck in there to give your writing a fake self-importance or to avoid saying anything too definite.

• Tone

Writing unaffectedly doesn't mean that you should use words and phrases such as 'okay', 'sort of' and 'a bit of a downer' in essays, even if their meaning seems as clear as day to you. A general use of slang would soon lead to . . .

• Imprecision

Do you know *exactly* what you mean? In the academic world it isn't good enough to get the general drift. Tighten up!

23

Use of English

• **Ignorance**

a. Check the meaning of any words in the question that you're unsure of; and *b.* avoid those intoxicating words that you don't properly understand but which seem to suggest a desirable depth and vision.

• **Spelling**

Tutors can get really screwed up about bad spelling - not because they're good at it themselves, but because they know it's the easiest job in the world to look things up.

> I said it in Hebrew - I said it in Dutch
> I said it in German and Greek;
> But I wholly forgot (and it vexes me much)
> That English is what you speak!
>
> *Lewis Carroll*
> *'The Hunting of the Snark'*

• **Passive constructions**

Strangely common timorousness. Don't write *Spinach was eaten by Popeye*, but (active) *Popeye ate spinach*. Not *It is claimed by the authors of the report*, but *The authors of the report claim*. Fall into the habit and you're done for.

• **Sexist language**

What, you? But some tutors will dock marks left, right and centre if you write: *A growing child should eat his food*. You can't pepper your essay with 'his/her', so find another way of putting it: perhaps the plural *(Growing children must eat their food)* or - though it offends grammatical purists - *a growing child should eat their food*.

• **Sentences run together.**

This one is breeding fast. Separate sentences may be joined by conjunctions such as 'and', 'but', 'although' and so on, but NEVER by a comma. The common practice of running them together is a bar to understanding and will lose you marks heavily. This is a sentence: *Popeye lusted after spinach.* So is this: *He ate it all the time.*

Note that each has its own subject and its own verb. Each happily stands by itself as a complete statement.

If you want to join them together to give your writing a better flow, the following is permissible:

Popeye lusted after spinach and / so (etc) he ate it all the time.

This, however, is NEVER allowed:

Popeye lusted after spinach, he ate it all the time.

Examine your own writing. If this is what you do: DON'T!

As if all that reading and writing wasn't enough, now you have to annotate the blessed essay, too

How to give credit where it's due

Since, as you now know, originality lies in marshalling the material that you've doggedly amassed, you shouldn't be nervous about revealing where it's come from.

In fact, not to come clean is regarded as at best slapdash and at worst barefaced cheating, so it's vital that you get it right.

Commonplace remarks or ideas *(Popeye was the stereotype of the muscular American sailor)* don't need to be attributed to anyone, but just about everything else does.

There is, unhappily, no single standard method of organising your reference material, but although the various disciplines have different approaches, there's a general tendency towards using the social sciences format, which is also known as the Harvard style. That's the system we've adopted here.

As a general rule, give the source of any quotations in parenthesis within the sentence and let the writing flow.

If the length of the quotation makes that approach impossible, however, break off and give the passage its own indented paragraph within the essay - still with the necessary information in brackets at the end.

> **"Notes are often necessary, but they are necessary evils."**
> **Dr Johnson**
> **'Preface to Shakespeare'**

Sometimes the nature of the material (or the demands of your tutor) will require those notes at the foot of the page or in a separate list at the end of the essay. The chief message here is that you should be thorough and consistent.

Our handy checklist on the next page should serve you well unless your tutor has a preference for some other system. Our advice is to ask at the outset.

References: the Good Essays Harvard-style checklist

- Direct quotations: not too many or too long
Do use: when an author makes a point far more stylishly and/or concisely than you can
Don't use: for common knowledge; obvious points

- Indirect quotations (paraphrases)
Do use: for original ideas or facts in your texts
Don't use: for common knowledge

- The source of all tables, maps, diagrams etc should also be acknowledged.

REFERENCES IN THE TEXT

- Direct quotations should appear in single quotation marks with a reference (including page number) in parenthesis: **As Smailes (1983: 145) has written, 'a phrase worth quoting' or 'Something I could not put better myself'** (Norme, 1994: 27).

- Indirect or paraphrased quotations also need a reference: **Peacock (1994) argued that this view was mistaken.**

- 'Second-hand' quotations must be acknowledged: **'only acceptable if you cannot consult the original source yourself'** (Smailes, 1983, cited in Peacock, 1992: 106).

- Two authors: **(Smailes and Peacock, 1985).**

- More than two authors: **(Smailes et al., 1994: 220).** But give their names in full in the list of references/bibliography.

- For an omission from a quotation use . . .

- To show an interpolation use square brackets: **[your own words, if you change something in the quotation slightly]**

LIST OF REFERENCES/BIBLIOGRAPHY

- All books or articles cited in the text should appear in the bibliography.

- No entries should appear in your bibliography that have not been cited in the text. If you've read it, cite it!

- Information needed:
Name of author and/or editor; year of publication; title of article/chapter in quotation marks; title of book or journal in italics; publisher and place of publication for books; volume number for academic journals; page numbers for articles/chapters.

- Entries appear in alphabetical order by surname of the first author/editor. This name is reversed: **Smailes, E.** not E. Smailes.

- Books:
Smailes, E., W. Peacock and S. Norme (1994) *The Art of Essay Writing*, Partridge Publishers, Edinburgh.

- Edited books:
Peacock, W. and E. Smailes (eds) (1982) *Essays on Essays*, Writers Press, Longstone.

- Chapter in an edited book:
Norme, S. (1993) 'Fifty years of teaching essay writing', in W. Peacock (ed.) *The English Essay: A Tradition Reviewed*, Thoroughgood, London, 22-47.

- Article in an academic journal:
Smailes, E. (1995) 'Why we need to write about writing', *Essays*, 3, 1, 98-117.

THE INTERNET

- References in text
Use the name of the author/organisation and the date on which the item was written: **(World Bank, 1997).**

- List of references
Include the URL of the site from which you obtained the material and the date on which you accessed it: **World Bank (1997) 'World Bank agrees to Itaparica Irrigation Project', Washington DC, World Bank** (http://www.worldbank.

By the early 1990s the Local Government Programme represented at best a deconcentration of decision-making rather than a true territorial decentralisation, because local delegations of the federal ministries and the provincial governments retained discretion in their approval of funding proposals. No public justification of expenditure decisions was required or given. Allocation was not transparent and reinforced political centralism.

An extract from Norme (1994: 37)

The Local Government Programme came to represent at best a deconcentration of decision-making instead of a 'true territorial decentralisation' (Norme, 1994: 37). In the early 1990s, the local delegates of federal ministries still retained discretionary powers in the approval of funding proposals, as did provincial governments. There was no public justification of how spending decisions were made. Allocation was far from transparent and political centralism was reinforced.

Failed student essay

When borrowing becomes theft

Study those two paragraphs at the top of the page and you'll probably feel some sympathy for the student who wrote the second one - and who was failed for plagiarism.

Plagiarism is regarded as a pretty serious academic offence, and (like being drunk in charge of a bicycle) it's all too easy to commit unawares.

Our unhappy student, being both honest and conscientious, was angry to be failed, and is to this day still shaking her intelligent head.

What had she done wrong?

Let's begin with what she *hadn't* done. She hadn't produced a single line or a single thought that wasn't directly influenced by the book she had read.

She hadn't either compared what Norme had to say on the subject with what other authors thought, or produced examples or statistics from elsewhere to show that Norme's analysis was a good one.

Yes, she'd acknowledged that the words in quotation marks were Norme's - but without letting on that the previous phrase came from Norme, too.

Yes, she'd paraphrased what she'd found in the book (a little) - but the important points were still the same. She'd added nothing, and she relied much more on Norme's words than she admitted.

In short, her tutor was being asked to assess Norme's work, not hers!

27

We're back to the subject of your originality.

Of course you know far less than a Norme and his professorial colleagues, and you're bound not only to consult the books they write but to make intensive use of their ideas. It's how you do it that counts!

We give below (with, as you would expect, full credit to the author) four examples of dealing with your source material.

Marx out of 10

In which University College London lecturer **Richard Dennis** brings us his unique Good Essays guide to plagiarism

 A

The history of all hitherto existing society is the history of class struggles. Society as a whole is more and more splitting up into two great hostile camps, into two great classes directly facing each other: Bourgeoisie and Proletariat. Masses of labourers, crowded into the factory, are organised like soldiers. Not only are they slaves of the bourgeois class, and of the bourgeois State; they are daily and hourly enslaved by the machine, by the overlooker, and, above all, by the individual bourgeois manufacturer himself. The proletarians have nothing to lose but their chains. They have a world to win.

> Marx out of 10: NIL.
> Dennis note: This is plagiarism. There is no attempt to indicate that these are not my own thoughts but are words taken direct from different parts of *The Communist Manifesto*.

 B

Marx and Engels noted that the history of all hitherto existing society had been the history of class struggles. Society as a whole was more and more splitting up into two great hostile camps, into two great classes directly facing each other: Bourgeoisie and Proletariat. They observed that proletarians had nothing to lose but their chains. They had a world to win.

> Marx out of 10: NIL
> Dennis note: This is still plagiarism. Although the ideas are attributed to Marx and Engels, there is no indication that the form of words is not mine. Just changing it into the past tense doesn't make it original.

Plagiarism

To summarise: what you *must* do, if you're to avoid the plagiarism charge, is to show that you've assimilated those ideas, giving them words, and a structure, of your own.

Yes, you can quote their works to illustrate the points you wish to make, but be sure to demonstrate that you have incorporated their thoughts in the development of your own individual argument.

In *The Communist Manifesto*, Marx and Engels (1973 edn., p. 40) noted that 'The history of all hitherto existing society is the history of class struggles'. They argued that society was 'more and more splitting up into two great hostile camps, into two great classes directly facing each other: Bourgeoisie and Proletariat' (p. 41). 'Masses of labourers, crowded into the factory' were 'organised like soldiers...slaves of the bourgeois class, and of the bourgeois State' (p. 52). They concluded that 'The proletarians have nothing to lose but their chains. They have a world to win' (p. 96).

> Marx out of 10: TWO
> Dennis note: This is not plagiarism, but if all your essay consists of is a set of quotations stitched together, it doesn't suggest that you have thought about or understood the contents of the quotations. A poor effort.

In one of the most famous first sentences ever written, Marx and Engels (1973 edn., p. 40) began *The Communist Manifesto* thus: 'The history of all hitherto existing society is the history of class struggles'. They went on to exemplify this claim by showing how the structure of society had, in their view, developed into two interdependent but antagonistic classes: bourgeoisie and proletariat. The latter comprised factory operatives, who had been reduced to no more than slave labour; but as they became concentrated geographically, in the great factory towns of the industrial revolution, so they had the opportunity to organise themselves politically. Hence, the authors' conclusion that a communist revolution was not only desirable but possible, leading them to issue their equally famous final exhortation (p. 96): 'WORKING MEN OF ALL COUNTRIES, UNITE!'

> Marx out of 10: FIVE
> Dennis note: This may not be a very profound commentary, but at least I've tried!

Index